The Portfolio Approach to Assessment

by
Emily Grady

Library of Congress Catalog Card Number 92-61018
ISBN 0-87367-341-7

Bloomington, Indiana

This fastback is sponsored by the St. Louis Missouri Chapter of Phi Delta Kappa, which made a generous contribution toward publication costs.

The chapter sponsors this fastback in honor of Dr. Louis Kittlaus, a 50-year member whose contributions to the fraternity and to the St. Louis Public Schools reflect his enthusiasm for and commitment to public education.

Table of Contents

Introduction

Measuring progress toward the education goals is far more complicated than administering a national test.

– Keith Geiger, President, NEA

Imagine that you are a grandparent, and you see your grandson only during monthly visits. One observation you are bound to make – in fact, exclaim over as each month passes – is how much the baby has grown. What would you mean by growing? Of course, you will notice that he seems heavier when you pick him up and that his toes are pressing the seams of the rompers you bought him just last month. You can weigh him on a scale or stretch out a tape measure and verify these facts, chart them on a growth curve, and compare him to other infants in his age range. You will have a good idea if he is increasing in length and gaining weight appropriately.

But there are many other ways the baby is growing. One month he sleeps in your arms and grips your finger tightly; the next month he may gaze intently into your eyes. As time progresses, he babbles and smiles; and you swear he recognizes you and responds differently to you than he does to others. Can you measure these changes with any kind of standard measurement like you did his weight and height? Can you say that his babbling has increased in standard increments? Can you rate him on a smile scale? Probably not, but you can record these signs of growth in other ways.

No doubt you have photo albums documenting his moods and milestones. You have tucked a tiny black curl tied with a ribbon into an envelope. You have written letters to friends describing his antics. You have commented to anyone who will listen how alert he is, how he calms to your crooning of "Good Night, Irene" faster than anyone else's attempts to lull him to sleep. You know many things about this baby, and these bits of information structure how you respond to him.

When teachers are entrusted with the education of children, they use similar methods of ensuring learning. They come to know how each student learns best: who should not sit by whom if a reading lesson requires concentration, or who will be frustrated by a page of addition problems but can handle the same work in small increments. Teachers also can look at test scores and know how their class compares with a national norm in basic math skills or reading comprehension. All of these pieces of information work together to give a complete picture of student progress.

Our students deserve to be treated like real people, not ciphers within a stanine. There are no standard kids; why should we assume that our evaluation of them should be standardized? The scores we get from norm-referenced tests are only one bit of information we can know about our students. They are valid but should not be used for purposes for which they are not suited. It is time to open the "portfolio" and present a complete picture of a child's learning.

Educators have long used performance or portfolio assessment: hands-on evaluation in vocational programs, essay assessments in advanced placement exams, performances or exhibitions in the arts. In fact, outside the United States, direct assessment of student performance is the norm rather than the exception. This fastback will analyze the shortcomings of standardized testing as the predominant form of student assessment in the United States and then examine the use and potential benefits of an alternative approach called portfolio assessment.

Testing in the United States

Ever since intelligence tests began to be widely used in the military service during World War I, the schools followed suit by using norm-referenced tests to assess student performance. By the 1930s millions of tests were being sold to schools every year, and their use has increased steadily over the ensuing years.

The Sputnik-induced reforms in the 1950s called for more testing, as did the reforms in the 1960s. The wave of reforms in the past two decades has resulted in minimum competency tests now being given in 42 states as graduation prerequisites. National exams became the crux of the Education 2000 plan proposed by President George Bush in 1991.

The desire to know in quantifiable terms exactly what our students have learned is a peculiarly American trait, but there seems to be little correlation between testing and producing successful students. American students are among the most tested yet academically deficient in the industrialized world. According to many educators and psychologists – even the head of Educational Testing Service – standardized tests just do not pass muster as a method of improving student performance. In fact, they may be undermining the very purpose they were intended to serve.

The American dependence on testing may reflect our strong faith in science; we equate objective data with truth. The use of tests as an accountability measure assumes that the learning process can be reduced to clear-cut goals and definable outcomes. This concept was seen at its extreme in the Sixties and Seventies, when broad learning goals were broken into incremental behavioral objectives, quantifiable skills that students were expected to learn in a prescribed sequence. This technical approach to learning made so-called objective measurements seem scientific and valid. One could make the numbers balance from the beginning to the end of the learning process.

Implicit in this technological framework is that scientific measurement is more reliable than professional judgment. This devotion to scientific measurement sent the message to teachers that, "Your professional evaluation is not good enough. Your experience and professional judgment are not as reliable or accurate as a page of circles blackened with #2 lead pencils."

Shifting authority from the professional educator to the testing industry may be doing more than harming the psyches of teachers. While standardized tests initially were created to measure student achievement in a simple, quantifiable, and inexpensive way, in practice they have taken on a much more influential role. Tests now are used to measure facts, skills, aptitudes, attitudes, and achievements. Students' scores have been used to fire superintendents, gain merit pay for teachers, and even set property values by using student achievement scores to rate local schools.

Because tests scores are used as public measuring sticks of a school district's worth, standardized tests are driving the curriculum. The teacher's role is reduced to that of a technician preparing students for tests, rather than that of a skilled professional guiding student learning. Such skills as critical thinking and problem solving are pushed into the background in favor of facts that are easy to test. The National Council of Teachers of Mathematics (NCTM) recognized this when they concluded in 1989 that math instruction cannot improve without a change in assessment procedures.

Children's educational experiences, and therefore their future job prospects and standard of living, are being decided by test scores.

Labeling, tracking, and decisions about retention often are based on standardized tests, sometimes before a child has even entered kindergarten. Moreover, standardized tests may be unfair or biased against some students. Their reliability is not uniform across cultures or even among different testers or test situations. This bias becomes a self-fulfilling prophecy. As Vito Perrone states, "When children are labeled 'unready' or 'slow learners' because of standardized test results, their educational opportunities become narrow, uninteresting, unchallenging" (Perrone 1991).

Instead of more tests we need a new attitude toward assessment, one that encompasses a variety of measurements. Gregory Anrig, President of Educational Testing Service, said in 1986: "Tests provide useful but limited information. . . . As tests concern the individual child, one must be careful not to put too much weight on them apart from other evidence of learning." In 1977 the NEA published *Alternatives to Standardized Testing* (Quinto and McKenna 1977), which endorsed such alternative forms of assessment as "professional judgment, samples of student work, contracts with students, interviews, teacher made tests and criterion referenced tests."

Portfolio assessment can be an encompassing format for this philosophy. Student performance, teacher observation and evaluation, self-assessment, and standardized scores can all shed light on a student's learning profile. We know there are many ways to learn. It is time we applied that tenet to evaluation of students. It is time we allowed ourselves and encouraged others to rely on professional judgment.

Portfolios in Use

The word portfolio brings to mind an image of an artist carrying a large black case with samples of work to show to a prospective client. That is very much what portfolio assessment is like. Students maintain collections of their best work as a representation of their academic success.

The most obvious benefit of this type of assessment is that most of the contents of the portfolio are actual pieces of student work, not approximations supplied by a score on a standardized test. However, portfolio-based assessment has other effects that make this form of evaluation educationally sound.

First, students have a vested interest in the creation of their portfolios, certainly more than they have for a file of test scores in the main office. The portfolio represents a range of efforts and tangible achievements; it presents a learning history. In a well-designed portfolio system, the student selects the pieces of work to be included in the portfolio. The student has the chance to revise it, perfect it, evaluate it, and explain it. It is different from work completed just to fulfill an assignment or written only for the teacher's eyes; a piece created for the portfolio bears a piece of the student's identity. Whether the work is a self-generated word problem in math or a persuasive essay, the student claims ownership. It represents the student in a concrete and authentic way that a stanine score cannot do.

When a portfolio is part of ongoing classroom activity, assessment models the natural rhythm that learning takes in the real world. In the real world, the production of something is followed by an assessment. The product is then revised on the basis of that assessment, and the revision is assessed. After assessing the revision, a final product is produced. The creation of a portfolio reflects that real-world process, in contrast to the manipulative, lesson-test model reflected by standardized tests. With portfolios, assessment is an important part of the learning cycle, rather than being merely a result.

A standardized test may show students in the 80th percentile for reading comprehension. The superintendent can look at that score and know that the teaching of reading is progressing well in the district. Legislators can look at the numbers and assume that things seem to be under control. Parents can feel secure that the district is educating their children. However, these good feelings do nothing to help the children learn to read or help the teachers who are teaching them. Individual strengths and weaknesses are not identified. In contrast, performance-based assessment lets students and teachers know exactly what needs exist. Students receive immediate feedback, gain confidence by acknowledgments of their strengths, and gain insight into how to improve. And teachers' professional skills in direct observation and evaluation are emphasized in a way that is missing from test-driven curricula.

Learning theory supports portfolio-based assessment. Humans do not accumulate skills and facts in a neat and orderly fashion. Strength in one skill may not mean that the connective activity of combining and using skills is taking place, just as a demonstrated weakness in a specific skill may not reflect why a student is misapplying the skill. Current learning theory also recognizes that there is a wide diversity in the pace and style of development among children and among cultures. By personalizing assessment, portfolios create a structure for individualized learning. Portfolio assessment also supports such teaching methods as whole language, process writing, thematic math and science, and collaborative learning.

Purposes and Standards for Portfolios

Before considering what a student portfolio should contain, it is important to establish the purpose of the assessment. An individual teacher can incorporate portfolios in one subject, or a whole school could adopt a portfolio system as a progress report to replace the traditional report cards. An entire district or even a state, as Vermont is now attempting, may adopt portfolios as a comprehensive student evaluation. In each case the information that the portfolio contains will be different.

Since the fall of 1990, Vermont has been experimenting with supplementing standardized tests with portfolios of actual class work. In the first year, students in fourth and eighth grades in 138 schools compiled math and English portfolios, which were accompanied by their own and their teachers' evaluations. The program has met with the approval of students, teachers, and parents. One of the main reasons given for its success has been that the criteria on which the portfolios are evaluated have been constructed by teachers with the aid of students and evaluation specialists.

Contents of the portfolio should meet pre-established standards. If we want to produce students who know how to think, we have to assess the ability to think; if we want students to write, we need to assess real writing. The Vermont experience demonstrates that consistent standards – whether national, statewide, or within a district – make assessment pertinent and valid to a school system. For example, states could establish minimum competency standards that portfolios must verify.

Though many education organizations oppose a national test, many do support an assessment system based on national standards. The National Council of Teachers of English (NCTE) has proposed to have a first draft of language arts standards by November 1992. The NCTM has already published a highly endorsed list of standards. Each school district, even each school, could determine what constitutes a complete portfolio by using national standards to guide the structure.

Within a school, portfolios could serve as a system for student promotion from one grade level to another. Certain information in a portfolio could be passed to the next teacher, serving as a diagnostic tool and providing a consistent record of the learning pattern for each student. But regardless of how portfolios are to be used, the purposes for the portfolio and standards for evaluating them must be established first. Following are examples of guidelines for two subjects, mathematics and language arts, that a teacher can use when evaluating portfolios.

Guidelines for Mathematics

In *Assessment Alternatives in Mathematics*, Jean Stenmark (1989) offers a variety of models for evaluating student work. The teacher may go over these questions with a student or use them to initiate a conference, as a checklist, or as a framework for a written formal evaluation. The presentation to the student will depend on grade level and purpose of the assessment.

- Problem Comprehension. Can students understand, define, formulate, or explain the problem or task? Can they cope with poorly defined problems?
- Approaches and Strategies. Do students have an organized approach to the problem or task? How do they record? Do they

use tools (manipulatives, diagrams, graphs, calculators, computers, etc.) appropriately?

- Relationships. Do students see relationships and recognize the central idea? Do they relate the problem to similar problems they did previously?
- Flexibility. Can students try another approach if one is not working? Do they persist? Do they try something else?
- Communication. Can students describe or depict the strategies they are using? Do they articulate their thought processes? Can they display or demonstrate the problem situation?
- Curiosity and Hypotheses. Is there evidence of conjecturing, thinking ahead, checking back?
- Equality and Equity. Do all students participate to the same degree? Is the quality of the opportunities for participation the same?
- Solutions. Do students reach a result? Do they consider other possibilities?
- Examining Results. Can students generalize and prove their answers? Do they connect the ideas to other similar problems or to the real world?
- Mathematical Learning. Did students use or learn some mathematics from the activity? Are there indications of a comprehensive curriculum?
- Self-Assessment. Do students evaluate their own processing, actions, and progress? (Stenmark 1989, pp. 24-25)

Using the above list as a framework, a math class might break into groups and tackle a problem like this one Bonnie Frank presented to her fifth-grade class at the New City School in St. Louis, Missouri:

> Determine the cost of the song, "The Twelve Days of Christmas." Use any sources you need to arrive at prices and document your efforts. Remember that some items repeat (for example, the partridge in the pear tree is mentioned 12 times; count each of these times in

your cost). Deliver the bill to the class in a presentation and show how you arrived at the total.

Projects such as these drive the curriculum. When evaluated according to criteria, the teacher can see where students need strengthening and where they show growth. The information gathered from such projects helps to structure future projects, determine group composition, and indicate where specific mini-lessons might be needed. In addition, a portfolio of such work is a concrete and valid representation of the learning that takes place in a school year. Student efforts are not tossed into the waste bin like so many worksheets. Their work is not practice; it is the real thing.

Guidelines for Language Arts

While general comments may help students' writing as they produce successive drafts, specific criteria help them to be aware of the component parts of good writing. Breaking the components into sections helps students to evaluate their work and to gain confidence by acknowledging their areas of strength. Noticed areas of weakness might become the target areas on which a student directs his efforts on the next project. The following is a list of criteria designed for secondary students in a composition class using an "order of concern" structure (Krest 1987). It can be used as a teacher-response tool, in peer editing, and in self-assessment.

Assessment Guidelines for Essays

High Order of Concern (HOC)

- Thesis:

    Arguable opinion.
    Directly stated (which paragraph?) or implied.
    Precise.

- Organization:

  Paragraphs support thesis.

  Paragraphs are controlled by a topic sentence.

  Paragraphs follow a logical order.
- Development:

  Thesis is supported.

  All support is pertinent to the thesis.

  At least three examples or an extended example illustrates the thesis.

  Paragraphs are detailed (concrete and specific).

Medium Order of Concern (MOC)

- Sentences:

  Control of sentence structure (syntax is understandable, clear to the reader).

  Variation of sentence types (length, complex, simple).
- Language:

  Usage is correct.

  Point of view is consistent and appropriate.

  Concrete diction (strong verbs, *le mot juste*).
- Audience Awareness:

  Tone.

  Appropriate language/vocabulary (sensitive to gender and race).

  Opposing views considered.

Low Order of Concern (LOC)

- Grammar (verb usage, pronoun agreement, clear pronoun antecedents).
- Punctuation.
- Spelling.
- Effective introduction.
- Effective conclusion.

A set of criteria such as the one above can help students to improve their work over a semester. As a formal assessment instrument, the list of criteria can be used to evaluate the portfolio at determined periods, for example, at semester grading periods.

What Goes in a Portfolio?

Portfolio-based assessment can encompass a variety of means to document and evaluate student growth. Following are some procedures for accumulating information that can shed light on development. Many are based on a classroom teacher's ability to observe student growth and progress.

Teacher Observations

Brian Cambourne and Jill Turbill provided a framework for using observation to gather information for assessing students in whole-language programs. What they arrived at was what parents do: observe and interact with their children, all the while framing their observations with an implicit understanding of normal growth and development. Formalized as an evaluation model known as "responsive evaluation," this method draws on such disciplines as anthropology and ethnography. The evaluator's task is to gather information by responding to those being evaluated, "by talking to them, observing them in action, and collecting 'artifacts' or outcomes from the various situations observed" (Cambourne and Turbill 1990).

In the same way, teachers become evaluators when they interact with their students, elicit information from them, observe their behaviors, collect their work, and record and synthesize the information, all in response to established criteria. How this is done will vary from teacher to teacher, but it does require classroom organization with assessment in mind and structured opportunities where the teacher can become a distanced observer to student behavior. It also requires a commitment by the teacher to record observations and to do this based on an established set of criteria.

Observation techniques can be as simple as jotting notes in a journal or using a checklist of observable descriptors that can be ticked off periodically. The teacher can establish a schedule to be certain that each student is observed or make it a point to observe certain students on certain days, though all unusual or remarkable behaviors should be noted as they occur. The synthesis of this material, done at regular intervals, will supply meaning to the behaviors and serve to adjust the future activities the teacher provides for the student. In this type of a system, classroom management, learning activities, and assessment are equally important components of the instructional process.

Establishing a time to enter observations into the student's portfolio will make the record keeping more efficient and meaningful. Again, by establishing a personal system, the job more likely will be accomplished. Rather than making observations in a log that would need to be transcribed, comments could be made on adhesive labels that could be placed in folders quickly. Computerized maintenance would make this task more time efficient as well as allow easy retrieval of information.

Observations need not be written. If the equipment is available, video and audio recording are viable techniques, as is photography. Using a classroom computer for entry and retrieval can be a valid organizational tool. Software such as the *Grady Profile*, published by Aurbach and Associates, has been created to help compile and store teacher and student observations, record oral observations, and scan students' written or graphic work.

Teachers must take care to conform to established criteria when making observations, because observations do not carry the objective "authority" of standardized tests. The possibility of subjectivity creeps in whenever the human element, however appropriate, is part of an evaluative situation. Dated observations and documentation should corroborate any evaluation, especially one that may have such lasting consequences for a student as acceptance into a program or placement in a group or class. Nothing should be placed in a permanent portfolio that cannot be substantiated. Any subjective or potentially damaging information should be kept in a teacher's personal notes or ignored if not pertinent to the student's growth and development.

Collections of Student Work

It is important to designate a place to collect student work that is easily accessible to the student and the teacher. The student should be aware that the portfolio is his or hers, yet it is important that the "official" portfolio be considered a piece of school property. To that end, it may be wise to maintain two portfolios. One would be a "working portfolio," kept in the classroom and accessible to the student. The second would be a permanent portfolio kept by the teacher, which contains selected pieces of work, teacher comments, observations, behavioral checklists, and test scores. The permanent portfolio may even be kept as a permanent record, containing annual samples of student work representing established criteria.

The working portfolio or portfolios (there may be one for each subject) could contain all works in progress, samples of art work, math problems, collaborative projects, lists of books read, reports written, documentation of performances, quizzes, and any useful examples of student work. From the working portfolio would come the samples that illustrate the student's best representative work. This could be a culminating exercise in each grade as part of the annual year-end evaluation. The selection, revision, and evaluation of the portfolio's contents would be done by the student, peers, teachers, and possibly parents and would be part of the portfolio creation process.

Working portfolios can be structured so that progress over time is noted. A weekly or monthly sample of work can be entered, such as a writing sample or solution to a word problem. Dating the work will give a picture of the student's progress over time.

In addition, students could keep a journal or log of the skills they have learned or the information they have discovered. These can serve as valid points of reference over an academic career. Used as starting points for self-evaluation, they can provide concrete evidence of a student's progress and needs.

Self-Evaluations

While simply gathering information will document activity, it is necessary to reflect on this information periodically. The teacher, of course, will respond to student work to strengthen weaknesses and acknowledge success. But perhaps even more meaningful to the assessment process is self-evaluation by the student.

When students can discuss their work objectively with their teacher or ruminate about it in their portfolio logs, they are taking charge of their learning and becoming aware of what and how they learn. This awareness, or metacognition, helps students move from passive to active learning. In addition, the teacher can encourage evaluative thinking even at the earliest levels of schooling by helping students to think critically about their own work and that of their peers. Following are some questions used in a writing class to help students conduct their self-evaluations:

1. Look back over your work this semester and discuss the strategies you used for creating it. Think about specific essays. Which were easy for you? Which were most difficult? What have you learned about your methods this semester?
2. What do you like about your writing? What do you feel are your strengths? Be as specific as you can; cite essays if possible.

3. What are you dissatisfied with in your writing? What areas do you feel need improvement?
4. In what specific areas have you grown this semester?
5. Discuss your target paper. Why did you choose it? What did you do to it to revise it to make it representative of your best work?

Self-evaluation encourages students to revise their work and motivates them to take the initiative in conferring with the teacher and their peers. The students assume responsibility for their work and their learning.

Questionnaires

Direct questions or profiles can help teachers know students better and can inform them about learning styles and preferences that can direct growth. Knowing that a student might prefer group discussions to solo desk work can help the teacher plan activities that will benefit the student and affect assessment. More formal indicators of learning style, such as the Myers-Briggs Type Indicator for older students, can have a valid place in a student profile.

Questionnaires also can be used to involve parents in their children's education. Parents can be asked about the learning activities that occur at home: How many hours of television does the child watch? Do you read with your child? Where does he do his homework? What time does he go to bed? Including a profile of parents' opinions on how their children learn or what learning occurs at home will focus the parents' attention on their children's learning and invite parents' active participation.

Keeping a Personal Professional Portfolio

Many teacher education programs are using portfolios as assessment instruments for preservice teachers. Just as portfolios document growth and provide content for formal and self-evaluations for elementary and high school students, they can help student teachers develop as professional educators. In addition, the autonomy and self-insight derived from keeping a portfolio will help new teachers to establish and reinforce their own professional integrity.

As a professional tool, the portfolio can benefit both preservice and inservice teachers. For preservice teachers, the information gathered in a portfolio can help when seeking employment, just as portfolios serve people in other professions. Also, the modeling of a current educational practice will serve a student teacher when used later in the classroom.

Inservice teachers can benefit by keeping a portfolio as a record of professional growth, formal evaluations, and self-evaluation. Publications, committee work, and curriculum projects could be organized as a representation of a teacher's professional life. The continued growth supported by a personal portfolio can reinforce professional self-esteem and integrity. In addition, modeling a process that we expect of our students will provide insight into how and why it does or does not work.

Implementation and Management

Keeping portfolios for each student takes a lot of time. One of the initial reasons that standardized tests gained entry into schools was that the traditional forms of observation were becoming unwieldy in the burgeoning public school systems at the turn of the century. With today's budget crunching, asking that a personal portfolio be kept for each student may seem like piling straw on an already broken camel's back. Chasing paper has never been a favorite activity for teachers, and a portfolio system heaped on top of an already bureaucratic system of record keeping could seem like adding the role of "file clerk" to a teacher's job description.

Keeping portfolios requires conscientious management, both of time and materials. For portfolio assessment to work, it must not be seen as just something added to a teacher's already overburdened workload. Assessment must truly become part of the curriculum. Classroom management styles must be adjusted to give teachers the time and opportunity to observe and reflect on student growth. With portfolio construction, the teacher becomes less like a manager and more like a coach. Students have a reason for self-investment, because self-evaluation is such an integral part of the process.

Joan Simmons, an eighth-grade English teacher in Vermont, commenting in *The New York Times* on the effects of portfolio management in her class, said: "I make them wean themselves from me and, boy, is that difficult. As a teacher you have to be willing to give up control, give up being a talking head. But if you do, after a little confusion, the rewards are fantastic. Discipline problems go out the window and kids are engaged" (DeWitt 1991).

Technology also can help in managing a portfolio system. Video and audio recording will help the teacher make observations. Computers help in managing, storing, and retrieving data. A computer can eliminate the paper burden and allow students to keep the original copies of their work. In addition, computers can make it easier for different departments in a middle school or high school to collaborate; for example, when students are writing reports for a science class or measuring or weighing in an art class. Online help from the English department could reinforce writing across the curriculum. Schoolwide criteria could be maintained objectively and simply.

Conclusion

National standardized tests have been proposed as a primary strategy for education reform. However, standardized tests will not improve education. They do not provide useful information for educating children; they may lack validity and reliability in what they attempt to assess; they drive the curriculum in harmful ways; they lead to unfair labeling; and they discriminate among races and between genders. The rising tide of testing in the United States in the past few decades threatens to drown us in useless statistics.

Education needs accountability, but accountability must contribute to the growth of students. Assessment needs to be based in the classroom. Teachers must be central to the assessment process; they must be the documenters and reviewers of their students' learning. Students must enter into the assessment process in order to gain insight and confidence in controlling their own learning. Portfolio-based evaluation, which is grounded in current cognitive theory, can provide the framework for a new curricular structure that integrates assessment into the learning loop.

Instead of national standardized tests, there should be a national agenda to establish criteria that guide student learning. But just as teachers and students should be involved in assessment, so should they be involved in developing these criteria. The valid observations of classroom teachers should nourish this process as they do their students' development.

Trusting teachers to assume the role as primary observers makes them better teachers. As they become trained in observing their students, they will know them better and will know more about how they learn. The role of teacher will expand to that of student. In addition to the benefits this extended role will provide to schools, teachers will model behaviors that they expect their own students to exhibit, that of an active observer who collects and documents data and then evaluates and makes sense of it. What more could we ask of our students? How dare we expect less? Why allow the paltry number of possibilities on a multiple-choice test to dictate the what and how of learning? Let's get real!

References

Anrig, Gregory. "Educational Standards, Testing, and Equity." *Phi Delta Kappan* 66 (May 1985): 623-25.

Anrig, Gregory, "Tests Can't Solve Every Problem." *U.S. News and World Report*, 19 May 1986, p. 84.

Aurbach, Richard, and Grady, Michael. *The Grady Profile: Portfolio Assessment*. St. Louis, Mo.: Aurbach & Associates Educational Software, 1991.

Belanoff, Pat, and Dickson, Marcia, eds. *Portfolios: Process and Product*. Portsmouth, N.H.: Boynton-Cook, 1991.

Cambourne, Brian, and Turbill, Jill. "Assessment in Whole-Language Classrooms: Theory into Practice." *The Elementary School Journal* 90 (January 1990): 337-49.

DeWitt, Karen. "Vermont Gauges Learning by What's in Portfolio." *The New York Times*, 24 April 1991, p. B7.

Gardner, Howard. "Assessment in Context: The Alternative to Standardized Testing." Prepared for the National Commission on Testing Policy, 1988. To appear in *Future Assessments: Changing Views of Aptitude, Achievement, and Instruction*, edited by B.R. Gifford and M.C. O'Connor. Boston: Kluwer Academic Publishers.

Krest, Margie. "Time on My Hands: Handling the Paper Load." *English Journal* 76 (December 1987): 37-42.

Perrone, Vito, ed. *Expanding Student Assessment*. Fairfax, Va.: ASCD, 1991.

Quinto, Frances, and McKenna, Bernard. *Alternatives to Standardized Testing: A Handbook*. Washington, D.C.: National Education Association, 1977.

Resnick, Daniel P., and Resnick, Lauren. "Standards, Curriculum, and Performance: A Historical and Comparative Perspective." *Educational Researcher* 14 (April 1985): 5-21.

Stenmark, Jean Kerr. *Assessment Alternatives in Mathematics*. EQUALS. Berkeley: University of California Regents, 1989.

Wiggins, Grant. "A Response to Cizak." *Phi Delta Kappan* 72 (May 1991): 700.